THE SENSES

# The Sense of Hearing

by Mari Schuh

Consultant:
Eric H. Chudler, Ph.D.
Director, Neuroscience for Kids
University of Washington
Seattle, Wash.

Note to Librarians, Teachers, and Parents:

**Blastoff! Readers** are carefully developed by literacy experts and combine standards-based content with developmentally-appropriate text.

**Level 1** provides the most support through repetition of high-frequency words, light text, predictable sentence patterns, and strong visual support.

**Level 2** offers early readers a bit more challenge through varied simple sentences, increased text load, and less repetition of high frequency words.

**Level 3** advances early-fluent readers toward fluency through increased text and concept load, less reliance on visuals, longer sentences, and more literary language.

**Level 4** builds reading stamina by providing more text per page, increased use of punctuation, greater variation in sentence patterns, and increasingly challenging vocabulary.

**Level 5** encourages children to move from "learning to read" to "reading to learn" by providing even more text, varied writing styles, and less familiar topics.

Whichever book is right for your reader, Blastoff! Readers are the perfect books to build confidence and encourage a love of reading that will last a lifetime!

This edition first published in 2008 by Bellwether Media.

No part of this publication may be reproduced in whole or in part without written permission of the publisher. For information regarding permission, write to Bellwether Media Inc., Attention: Permissions Department, Post Office Box 1C, Minnetonka, MN 55345-9998.

Library of Congress Cataloging-in-Publication Data
Schuh, Mari C., 1975–
  The sense of hearing / by Mari Schuh.
     p. cm. — (Blastoff! readers: the senses)
  Summary: "Introductory text explains the function and experience of the sense of hearing. Intended for grades two through five"—Provided by publisher.
  Includes bibliographical references and index.
  ISBN-13: 978-1-60014-070-9 (hardcover : alk. paper)
  ISBN-10: 1-60014-070-X (hardcover : alk. paper)
  1. Hearing—Juvenile literature. I. Title.

QP462.2.S36 2008
612.8'5—dc22                                        2007022847

# Contents

# Your Sense of Hearing

What's that sound? All day long, you use your sense of hearing to learn about your surroundings.

You listen carefully to your teacher. You hear a dog bark. Noisy cars zoom down the street. You hear your favorite song on the radio.

Hearing is one of your senses. Your other senses are sight, touch, taste, and smell.

# How Hearing Works

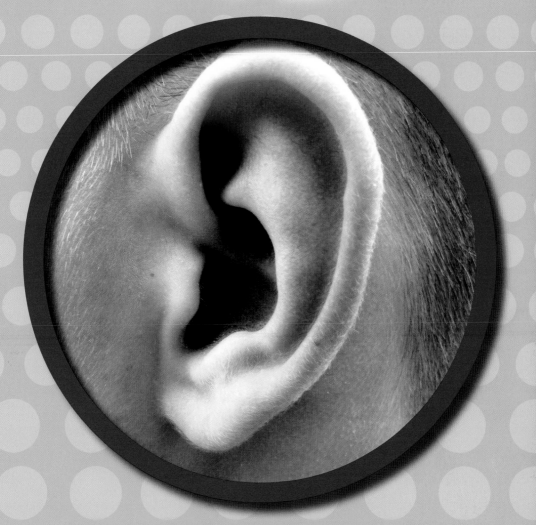

Your ears have three main parts. They are the outer ear, the middle ear, and the inner ear. Your ears and brain work together to help you hear sounds.

Sounds move through the air as **sound waves**. They travel to your outer ear. The outer ear is the part of the ear you can see. Your outer ear catches sound waves and moves them into your **ear canal**.

! **fun fact**

Your brain hears many sounds every day. But you don't remember them all. That's because your brain doesn't tell you about sounds that aren't important. This means you can focus on the sounds you need to hear.

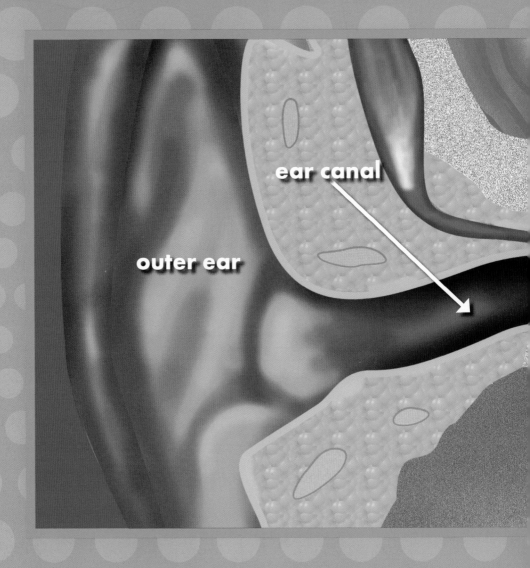

**ear canal**

**outer ear**

The ear canal leads to your **eardrum**. Your eardrum is in your middle ear. Sound waves make the eardrum **vibrate**.

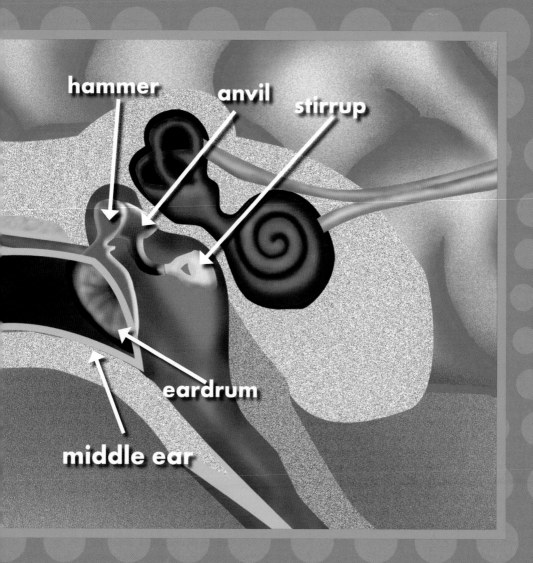

hammer
anvil
stirrup
eardrum
middle ear

The vibrations of your eardrum move three tiny bones in your middle ear. These bones are called the **hammer**, the **anvil**, and the **stirrup**. Their movements send the vibrations deeper into your ear.

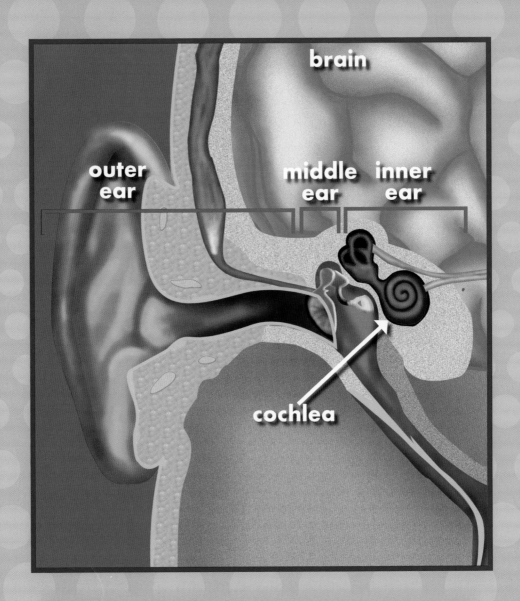

brain

outer
ear

middle
ear

inner
ear

cochlea

The vibrations travel to your inner ear and reach a curly tube called the **cochlea**.

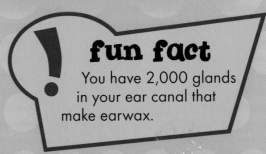

**fun fact**

You have 2,000 glands in your ear canal that make earwax.

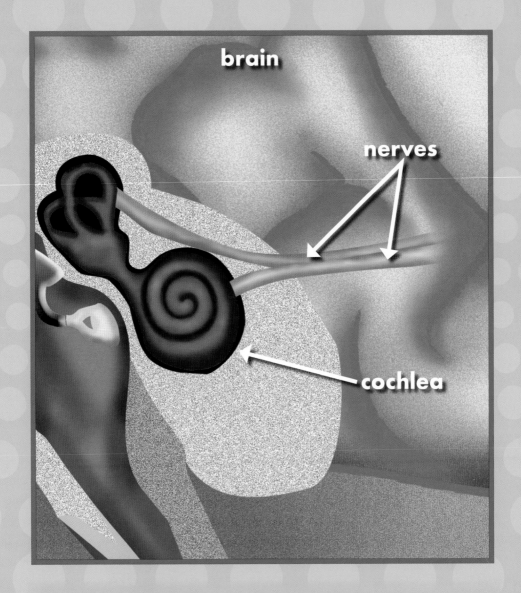

Small hairs on the cochlea move. The hairs connect to thin strings of tissue called **nerves**. The nerves send a message to your brain. You hear the sound when the message reaches your brain.

# Types of Sound

Some sound waves move faster than others. Sound waves that move quickly have a high **pitch**. Whistles make a high-pitched sound.

Sounds such as whispers are very soft. You need to be quiet to hear them. Other sounds are so loud you can't hear anything else. Planes taking off from a runway can be very loud.

## fun fact

Children usually have better hearing than adults.

# Animals and Hearing

Many animals use their sense of hearing to stay safe. Squirrels can hear the rustling of leaves as a predator moves closer.

Dogs have a great sense of hearing. They can hear sounds that people can't hear at all.

# Hearing and Safety

Loud noises can hurt your ears. Workers wear earplugs to keep loud sounds from entering their ears.

Listening to loud music can damage your ears too. Always listen to music at a low volume.

**fun fact**

Ears help you hear, but they also help you keep your balance.

Sounds can warn you of danger.
Sirens warn you there is an emergency.
A smoke alarm tells you there is a fire.

Your sense of hearing allows you to hear a cheering crowd. You can listen to music and hear your friends on the phone. What sounds do you hear right now?

# Glossary

**anvil**—one of three bones in the middle ear

**cochlea**—a curved tube in your inner ear; the cochlea helps send messages to your brain about the sounds you hear.

**ear canal**—the narrow tunnel from your outer ear to your eardrum

**eardrum**—a thin membrane inside your ear that vibrates when sound waves hit it

**hammer**—one of three bones in the middle ear

**nerves**—thin strings of tissue throughout your body; nerves carry messages between your brain and other parts of your body.

**pitch**—the tone of a sound; low sounds have a low pitch and high sounds have a high pitch.

**sound wave**—a series of vibrations in a gas, liquid or solid; the vibrations can enter the ear and be heard as sound.

**stirrup**—one of three bones in the middle ear

**vibrate**—to move back and forth very quickly

# To Learn More

**AT THE LIBRARY**
Barraclough, Sue. *What Can I Hear?* Chicago, Ill.:
Raintree, 2005.

Gray, Susan Heinrichs. *The Ears*. Chanhassen, Minn.:
Child's World, 2006.

Mackill, Mary. *Hearing*. Chicago, Ill.: Heinemann,
2006.

Pryor, Kimberly Jane. *Hearing*. Philadelphia, Pa.:
Chelsea, 2004.

Rau, Dana Meachen. *Shhhh...: A Book about
Hearing*. Minneapolis, Minn.: Picture Window Books,
2005.

**ON THE WEB**
Learning more about hearing
is as easy as 1, 2, 3.

1. Go to www.factsurfer.com

2. Enter "hearing" into search box.

3. Click the "Surf" button and you will see a list of
   related web sites.

With factsurfer.com, finding more information is just a
click away.

# Index

The images in this book are reproduced through the courtesy of: Paulaphoto, front cover; Nick Clements/ Getty Images, pp. 4-5; Lisa Pines/Getty Images, p. 6; Sergey Kogun, p. 7; Steve Satushek,/Getty Images, pp. 8-9; Linda Clavel, pp. 10, 11, 12, 13; Tomas Adel/agefotostock, p. 14; Sharply_Done, p. 15; Chris Rokitski, p. 16; GK Hart/Vikki Hart/Getty Images, p. 17; Dennis MacDonald/agefotostock, p. 18; Tim Mantoani/Masterfile, pp. 19, 21; Kevin Penhallow, p. 20.